The Rock Wall

Written by Simon Mugford

This is a rock wall.

Can you get to the top of it?

You will need this kit.

rope

helmet

harness

Grip the rock with your hands.
Look up.

Pull with your arms.
Up you go!

Put your feet on the rock wall.
Bend your knees and push up.

The rope will keep you safe.

You are at the top of the rock wall.
You can look down now!

Go back down and land on the mat.
Good job!

Talk about the book

Ask your child these questions:

1 Which three pieces of kit were needed to go up the rock wall?

2 Should you look up or down when you are climbing a rock wall?

3 Where did the child land when they went back down the wall?

4 Why was there a mat on the floor?

5 Have you ever been to a rock wall?

6 What is the highest thing you have ever climbed?